In Relation to the Surface: Poems

In Relation to the Surface: Poems

by

M. B. Powell

Cover Art: *Intrigue*
by Helen Saunders, Camano Island, Washington
(Helen Saunders Art at www.helensaunders.com)

ISBN: 978-1-949229-82-0

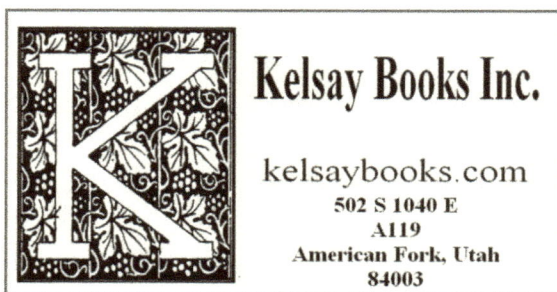

Kelsay Books Inc.

kelsaybooks.com
502 S 1040 E
A119
American Fork, Utah
84003

for Maureen

Acknowledgments

The author acknowledges the following journals, in which individual poems in this collection originally appeared: *America Magazine,* "Of the Tibetan Lion Dog"; *Atlanta Review,* "Phrases for Public Speakers at Sea"; *Aurora,* "Fish Spine" (as "Afterlife") ; *Dappled Things,* "One Zennish Adonic, Skin of a Bubble"; *Dogwood,* "Split Couplet on Same"; *J Journal: New Writing on Justice,* "Triolet on the Opening Lines of the Green River Killer's Holographic Apology for Killing Forty-Eight Women"; *Midway Journal,* "Helicon Cracking"; *Peregrine,* "A November Meditation on the Long Nave"; *The Raintown Review,* "Slack Water"; *Rock and Sling,* "Crucifixion Underwear"; and *Think: A Journal of Poetry, Criticism, and Reviews,* "Daphne, Repurposed."

Four poems originally appeared in the anthology of the Georgia Poetry Society, *The Reach of Song:* "About Playing House, I Can Tell You," "One Mother's Day," "Resolution," and "The VFW Post 3308 Cemetery." The poem "Open Houses" was originally published in the anthology *Sailing in the Mist of Time: Fifty Award-Winning Poems.*

The following poems originally appeared in the chapbook *Lovers, Mothers, Killers, Others* (Finishing Line Press, 2013): "Beginner, Interrupted, Attempting the Survival Float"; "Diana" (as "Actaeon"); "The Etymology of *Fathom* as a History of My History with You"; "The Littoral Zone"; "*Mold:* The Movie"; "One Brownie Starflash Moment in Black and White"; "The Only Ones"; "Séance, a Vision for the One Shipping Out"; and "Some Siberian Lake" (as "Castaway").

Any changes in the previously published poems are the author's own.

It goes down deeper than any anchor rope will go, and many, many steeples would have to be stacked one on top of another to reach from the bottom to the surface of the sea.
—Hans Christian Andersen, "The Little Mermaid," *Fairy Tales Told for Children* (1837)

Contents

I. Below

Phrases for Public Speakers at Sea

The student should read aloud daily several pages of these phrases, think just what each one means, and whenever possible fill out the phrase in his own words. A month's earnest practise of this kind will yield astonishing results.
—Grenville Kleiser, *Phrases for Public Speakers* (1910)

We ought, first of all, to note
      her oceanic eyes flecked with sea wrack.
And we should pause to consider
      the wavy wilderness of her damp hair.

I will not dwell on
      her cheeks ruddy under my thumbstrokes.
I will not attempt to explain
      the shapely, opalescent shells of her ears.

I wish to call your attention to
      the cunning animal of her mouth, muscular.
I wish to say something about
      the mollusky dark language of her kisses.

I am obliged to mention
      her sudden breasts, breaching, rhythmic.
And I am perfectly astounded at
      her finger charting my lips round her nipple.

Here, in this connection, let us notice
      the pressure against the roof of my mouth.
Here, in passing, let us observe
      her palms casting me down the dark seaway.

And here, I have to speak again of
      sea wrack, oceanic pools, salt waves.
And here, I wish I could stop
      and surface, save myself, return to tell.

But now it begins to be apparent
        that I am far weaker than I had thought.
And now we are naturally brought on to
        the sea change that deception brings.

You may point, if you will, to
        scripture, proverbs, and therapeutic talk.
You may also search through history
        and learn that my deafness is archetypal.

It is, to be sure, a melancholy fact that
        love's clouds will ever hang on us, drown us.
It is, to be sure, a notorious fact that
        love's tempest has driven me from my home.

What remains to be shown is
        whether I can put an end to this.
What remains to be considered is
        whether anyone should.

For when we contemplate
        the doldrums of life, we cannot rest.
And, likewise, when we reflect upon
        the pitiful port, we must rush into peril.

Let no one suppose
        I can tread safely the sea green of her eyes.
Let no one suggest there is any among us
        who could. I sink. I lose everything.

Permit me to illustrate the point:
        I am overboard, hands manacled in her hair.
Permit me to remind you that
        you have not met her, felt her undertow.

Diana

—after William Browne's "Song"

For her calves if she be running,
for her running, I admire her.
For her hands if she be bathing,
for her bathing, I attend her.

For her lips if she be smiling,
for her smiling, I do love her.
For her eyelids when she's sleeping,
for her sleeping, I must move her.

Lids, lips, hands, calves, everything
I see so commends her,
running, bathing, smiling, sleeping,
that for everything I desire her.

The Etymology of *Fathom* as a History of My History with You

Substantive. Dative. The arms embracing.
The lap, bosom, breast, or womb encasing.
In the *fathoms* of angels. In the *fathoms* of you.

Semantics. A weakening. The arms extended.
Recanted, their circle. A new width invented.
A wingspan. Six feet. The ambit of you.

Contraction. Abstraction. The handgrip, the power.
Conversion. Now action. To control, to devour.
In the *fathom* of fiends. Your fire *fathoms* me.

Semantics. A widening. The vise expanded.
A tract, a sweep. Then the noun's upended.
The deep. The *fathom*. The abyss of you.

Regression. A narrowing. A unit of measure.
Six feet of the deep. From surface to treasure.
The depth of a grave. My distance from you.

Conversion. A verbing. To sound, to determine
the depth of a body by sinking a plumb line.
To penetrate. Comprehend. As in, you *fathom* me.

Words Float Here

The room is weatherless,
antique chairs,
placid silk plants.

Words float here,
dust particles,
watercolors.

No snowfall, heatwave,
the room is weatherless,
nothing to remark.

Ignorant of gravity,
words float here,
incapable of weight.

Cloudbursts, blizzards,
all repressed,
this room is weatherless.

Static on the line
between us,
words float here.

Helicon Cracking

Your cadence makes me   crave rain,
the past-ripe grapeshot   of a grandstanding,
ill-bred downpour,   ignited by lightning,
drowning me in a blast   of bursting coins.

I'm sick of this metro-   sexual drizzle,
low-salt spa sheen   sweet-talking my skin,
christening me   a member of nothing,
just one more sleep-   walker on the sidewalk.

When will I hear   the white steed's
hooves on rock   and Helicon cracking,
the freed spring   speaking from the fissure?

Wasting away,   I am wasting away
on vapor, caution,   equivocation.
I need fire, Zeus,   not fog, not you.

Our Day in Couplets with Silent Refrain
[You were there, no matter where you were.]

Went downtown and tried on some shoes.
Read the *Stranger* at Starbucks or pretended to.
[. . .]

Drove to Golden Gardens and sat in my car.
Went down to the beach and sat some more.
[. . .]

Studied the Sound and the sound it made.
Went home for a while. No mail today.
[. . .]

Met a friend for dinner. Didn't eat, spoke less.
Got lost, got home. Stared at some heads.
[. . .]

Heard a noise, looked out. Nothing to see.
Drifted to bed and waited for sleep.
[. . .]

For My Steep Decline on I-5

I blame the sacrificial snowflakes defying mass and speed.
Nature, her careless ways.

I blame the voided minutes and miles of my solo commute south.
I blame Work, its upper hand.

I blame the hard-bitten harmonica in Springsteen's mouth.
Music, its presumptuous grip.

I blame the lost sight of the sun cracked across the Cascades.
I blame Life, its flashy promise.

I blame the evergreens, breaching the privacy of the naked birches.
I blame Some People, their nerve.

Then, too, I blame the birches, lungs frozen in the act of breathing.
I fault Frailty and Fear, mainly my own.

I blame yesterday's snow, untouched beneath the firs and cedars.
Nature, still, and, inevitably, Death.

Sad, too, the strands of taillights ahead, pulled from the Nisqually.
I blame Beauty, its illusion, and America, to some extent.

And then there's you, your ways, your hand, your grip.
I blame your promise and all that went before.

But mainly I blame myself, my nerve, and all that came after.
I blame my own inevitable death to some extent.

Some Siberian Lake

That last crevasse in my assault on Hope
took my breath away when it appeared,
but, headlong, ever the idiot mountaineer,
I pursue thin promises up that icy slope,
where one misstep, one bolt of truth, no rope
will hold, straight down I'll go, and down is where
I'll stay. She takes my sky away. Down there,
there is no periscope, no happy trope:
I'm trapped in a shaft of apparitional fish
a half-mile deep in some Siberian lake,
breathing a darkness no distant day can break.
I watch a few light out, crazed by a wish
to scale the depths. No use. Each bursts into
an oily drop atop the grotto blue.

The Littoral Zone

Headless speckosaurus, cold and slick,
its flipside flat, ripped into a tilde grin:
quirky choice to make when I was six,
that shell, and could have chosen, from that
or any other shop on the miraculous strip,
a flashier shell, one unfurling, pearly and pink.
Or I could have picked the showy starfish,
an inflatable seahorse for braving the waves,
or a sailor's hat, my name in glitter on the cuff,
but it seemed alive, that borderline ugly thing.
I stroked its glossy hide, strummed the ridges
on its underside, clamped its mouth to my ear,
and heard exactly what I was told I'd hear.

Decades later, at a gift shop on another coast,
my eyes light on a bin of cowry shells,
the polished plunder from some exotic shore.
I take the top one from the heap, my cheap
trip back disguised as a kitschy paperweight.
Back at our ocean-view studio, the din
of the Pacific out the sliders to my left,
I slip the shell from its plastic bag, admire
its heft in my right hand, and press it to my ear.
The sound of the ocean? What a joke. Against
the thrash of that incessant present, a faraway
highway is all I hear, or a breeze, its frail voice
sifting through the seams of an abandoned house.

So call it what you like—ossified womb,
dead egg, ceramic zipper, the snail long gone
behind it—but there's nothing metaphoric here.
This was a house built in the littoral zone,

on the sand between the tidemarks, high and low,
built to weather by turns the breaking waves,
the unmediated sun and wind. And for what?
All that effort to survive and thrive, to build
something lasting, and it will never be enough.
No matter how hard you've worked and planned,
things change or you do. People leave or you do.
I see what's in store: this bone house, this place
I made with you, my mainstay, quietly cast away.

Slack Water

ic æfre ne mæg
þære mod-ceare   minre gerestan . . . .
(My heart shall never
suddenly sail into slack water . . . .)
—"The Wife's Lament," ll. 39-40 (trans. Michael Alexander)

Should I ever say   (after a caesura, mine,
as a consequence of   the cutting off, yours),
                    I will never be able
to rest from my heartache,
please don't believe   my lamentation:
don't see my life   as some sorrowful passage,
one cold, unchanging   current in charge,
or imagine me   in the midst of the tempest,
seasick in the hapless   Sea Venture's hold.
All stiff tides turn   and storms abate.

See? There I stand   on the sunny deck
of a different ship,   a dive boat
idling in the waters   off the Azores.
The tide dissolving   to zero speed,
no silt rising   from a roiling seabed,
soon I'll be slipping   into slack water.

II. Near

Beginner, Interrupted, Attempting
the Survival Float

An ax blade
on a whetstone
distresses
the air

(hollow
aluminum
fretting coarse
cement,

as she springs
from the web
of her poolside
chair),

felling
the beginner
in the shallow
end.

Crucifixion Underwear

patent leather shoes like goathooves clicking
the rabbit-fur cape slightly slipping
the parasol a problem with the handbag whipping

(and another troublesome thing to clutch
the engraved Bible zippered shut)

organdy dress with its soft percussion
perpendicular skirt on its firm foundation
petticoat and crinoline's laceration

(and above the de rigueur carapace
not one curl is out of place!)

home to the photos between starched brothers
bow ties, rosebuds, slick white loafers
home to the eggs and their tasteless colors

(in your rococo halo of tortured hair
in your crucifixion underwear)

Mold: The Movie

1. Gertrude's Take

*"A few times when we have left the studio together, she has looked up at me
and said, 'Mommy, did I do all right?'* . . . *I have replied, noncommittally,
'All right.' That was the end of it."*
—Gertrude Temple, as qtd. in Anne Edwards, *Shirley Temple: American
Princess* (1988)

What it took to create that child was a grand design,
and by that I mean mine.
I envisioned her. I had the will to conceive.
And *knowing* she was there, not simply make-believe,
I devoted our 266 days to what she might perceive.
Twirling about the living room (the phonograph never idle),
I kept time with a tambourine, awaiting her arrival.
I attended every local band and dance recital.

What it took to create that hair was time,
and by that I mean mine.
Each weeknight, I took 56 strands (previously tinted),
twisted them into 56 perfect *O*s, and cemented
those in metal *X*s—thus was the a.m. halo reinvented;
and on Sunday mornings, still more work to do:
I brewed from a bar of laundry soap a stove-top shampoo,
endured an acrid vinegar rinse, and pinned her up anew.

What it took to create that smile was some spine,
and by that I mean mine.
I fashioned for her thumbs a pair of matching torques
from the wire cages housing champagne corks
(to stop that sloppy habit, you have to do what works!),

and in my alligator bag I carried the porcelain twin
of every baby tooth, a plate to trap the stand-ins in,
and, to snap a truant cap in place, dental powder in a tin.

What it took to create that star was a need to shine,
and by that I mean mine:
I had her swaying in her crib at eight months old,
taking tap at barely three at Ethel Meglin's Studio,
and within a year, burlesquing Dietrich and Garbo.
I taught her how to wet her lips and grow misty-eyed,
and, as each scene began, *Sparkle, Shirley, sparkle!*, I'd
command. She usually did all right. I was satisfied.

2. My Take

> *"Please send me a BB gun and a bicycle," I wrote, adding as a cautionary note, "I have too many dolls already." I got dolls, all sorts.*
> —Shirley Temple Black, *Child Star* (1989)

I got all sorts, too, and worst of all,
or so I thought then, I got you.
And yet, you were the one I saved, my sole
surviving vinyl foster child.

Saved? I took horrendous care of you.
In a plastic Rich's bag, inside
a cardboard box stored on a closet shelf,
I hid you away as if concealing

some shameful life mistake, left you there
for decades in the dark until it crossed
my mind that I could make a buck off you,
take you for a Roadshow critique

or cast you into eBay's harsh limelight
with the other Shirleys on display,
some mint, some nude, one nude and headless, too.
I turned an appraising eye on you

and saw you had it all, the crisp gold dress,
the crinoline, panties, socks, and shoes,
even the gold script pin and velveteen bow.
But when I took a harder look

and saw how shabbily Ideal, Time, and I
had treated you—your left leg shortened
so you could stand, an aqua mold allowed
to stipple your unprotected limbs,

your frayed socks pooling on your Mary Janes—
a deeper selfishness settled in.
I have to keep you here, frozen in jaunty
midstride atop my sunlit desk,

beaming, as the black mold grows on your tongue:
cruel memento, not of death but of me—
damaged, aging, yet still striving to please,
hoping to hear that I've done all right.

Mrs. America

*When the judges announced that Evelyn Joyce Schenk of New Jersey had
won the Mrs. America contest, the good news was too much for Mrs. Schenk.
She slumped to the platform in a dead faint and had to be revived before she
could be rewarded.*

*When the shouting dies down in Philadelphia, the chances are that either
Jersey Joe . . . will be on the floor or Rocky will.*
—Excerpts from *LIFE* (September 22, 1952)

What right-cross Susie-Q rocked you,

took the starch out of you,

mopped the floor with you,

left you lying there like a woman
shot in the act of giving up?
Was it the tiara nearing like a dish
of diamonds or one concussive flashback
to the punishing early rounds, you

attending the Stanley Hostess Parties
to ogle the Kitchen Utility Sets, you

bearing platters of crustless sandwiches
infused with Borden's cheese spreads
for those in your living room mesmerized
by the Philco High Fidelity set, you

stooping at the Hotpoint oven door
preparing to take the holiday turkey out,
your strand of Mikimotos swinging
across your mouth like a bit? With a jolt
of ammonia and perfume, you,

the genie of our house, are summoned,
our hourglass of the moment righted at last,
time flowing through you once again, you

still in fighting trim, strapped into Milady's
easy-on long-lined front-hook-uplift garment,
lightly boned for abdominal bulge, you

pumped up on your toes again, your seams
forever straight in your sixty-gauge
gloriously long-wearing Kayser's nylons
with the twist-resistant heel, you

embarking on your long walk down the runway
to nowhere but back again, soon to be
sailing home in the passenger seat of your
Dual-Range Pontiac or '52 Customline Ford,
your husband in suit and tie at the helm, you

alongside him in your city tweed suit
with velvet collar and ostrich-trimmed belt,
the two of you dressed perfectly fit to kill,
spinning along on the spotless life preservers
of your BF Goodrich whitewalls, useless.

Daphne, Repurposed

spectat inornatos collo pendere capillos,
et "quid, si comantur?" ait.
(He sees the loose disorder of her hair
And thinks what if it were neat and elegant!)
—Ovid, *Metamorphoses*, I.497-98 (trans. A. D. Melville)

Pursued past pallor to the river's edge
(Apollo's words heavy on her neck),
Daphne begs her rivergod father
to destroy her vexing beauty

(magnetic, despite the messy hair).
Unraveled feet grown graveward,
tangled hair woven to a green shock,
breasts boarded up—

she'll enliven no more lakes or rills,
this fully repurposed water nymph,
now anchored in the stony slope,
her loose disorder ordered.

See, Apollo, how neat and elegant she is?
Aromatic, ageless, largely motionless . . .

About Playing House, I Can Tell You

How we swept the barren patch at the far corner of our fenced
       backyard;
How we followed the lead of the First Little Pig, using the pine
       straw from the burn pile to lay out our house, modest, two-
       bedroom;
How we lived within our blueprint, drawn on the brown ground
       with needles, dry, the color of ants;
How we left gaps for doors, front, back, between the rooms;
How we could ignore the gaps and walk through the walls;
How we did so when we forgot about doors or were just over it,
       the whole thing;
How the entire enterprise rode on our imaginations;
How pedestrian our imaginations were, pokey, swaybacked;
How the girl next door, bossy, older, assigned roles, mother, father,
       children;
How it was rarely very much fun, no matter who you were;
How it was even less fun or none at all when you were alone inside
       with your cooperative dolls;
How their hard little eyes clicked open and shut, open and shut,
       depending;
How you always knew you could rake away the whole sad project
       with very little huffing and puffing;
How it could not compare to that afternoon at Cynthia's, the
       running over narrow paths through the thicket of a
       greenbelt behind the predictable apartments, the ropey
       vines to swing on, our heels grazing the forbidden, excited
       creek, the other children strangers to us, thrilling, the
       October wind on our arms and faces;
How it prepared me for days like that one, lives like this one.

On My Attempt to Capture Water in My Work
in Some New and Startling Way

*I'd decided that I wanted the pulse of the trees in my work, the journey of
grass, some dirt. I thought I might be able to capture water in some new and
startling way.*
—Artist Lara Liveman in Colum McCann's *Let the Great World Spin* (2009)

I'd decided that I wanted a flat, brown house in my work,
     flanked by a pair of pulseless trees.

I'd decided that I wanted the pulseless trees to stand
     in pools of dirt atop the go-nowhere grass.

I'd decided that I wanted my carpet of go-nowhere grass
     to lack magic, to be indoor-outdoor.

I achieved this effect by breaking Crayola Green,
     peeling it, raking it sideways. Smooooooth.

I'd decided that I wanted a face on the house in my work
     so plain it betrayed nothing at all,

so I centered a colorless door between crossless windows
     and bisected the lawn with a concrete neck.

My style was Prairie and Primitive (some would say Sad).
     I abandoned the classic elements: clouds;

the quadrant of yellow in the upper right corner,
     its dash-hyphen rays zapping the house;

the chimney and its sprung coil of solid smoke;
     the iconic Stick family holding Stick hands.

I'd decided that I wanted a blood-red river in my work,
      flowing due south from the base of the sky:

hence the fanning avalanche of hard-pressed Red,
      its pseudopodia menacing the house;

hence the Black crests carved in the clotted water,
      inverting the birds omitted from my sky;

hence my decision to rest, call the whole thing
      good, the world according to me.

One Brownie Starflash Moment in
Black and White

And the sun so bright
our eyes are just waking

and the sky stark white
like the ground

and our shadow selves
in vectors merging

like clock hands locked
on the frozen ground

and a power line streaking
from the northwest margin

stitching the back of your head
to the house

(and the house not our house
but a wintry port,

some stranger's summer home,
far from home)

and your hand on my shoulder:
may no future unhinge us,

no word crease the air— *"Elec-
tricity!"*—to unfreeze us,

release us from silence, from snow,
from strangeness,

from this sun so bright
our eyes are just waking.

One Mother's Day

Joyless Juliet in her Einstein hair
yowls like a cat from her third-floor balcony,
stopping strangers on the sidewalk below,
jerking us to our windows across the street,
disturbing our Sunday expectations.

From blocks away, just this side of the bridge,
the sirens are wailing, then whoosh they're here,
the patrol car, doors wide, radio on
with its affectless current of crises,
and the fire engine, brilliant, substantial.

Quiet now, the six-legged walking shadow
wonders vaguely who could be in such need,
watches as he alights from the engine,
Romeo in uni and latex gloves,
toting his toolbox full of solutions.

Last week, she wandered up the street alone,
her walker left behind. Grasping the top
of her neighbor's tall fence, hand over hand,
she climbed the long horizontal pole,
yapping at the wind in the steady rain.

Someone always comes along to save her,
some neighbor, some fool, some paid caregiver.
Even now, there is someone behind her,
talking with the EMTs, explaining
the bloody nightdress, the accusations.

Because he is so good with *words, words, words,*
she will stop worrying the impatiens
hanging overhead, fretting the dried leaves,
and follow, clutching bits of undergrowth,
touching with earthy fingertips her wound.

Yesterday, the daughters made their visit,
showed up with baskets of flowers, hard candy,
used their outside voices, overacting.
Now they will have this Sunday to themselves,
feted by their own theatrical children.

III. On

Reservoirs

[The Mona Lisa of the Loggia]
Behind her smile,   behind the fusty
pyramid of cloth   and pinned-on hands,
lies the promising,   postlapsarian
countryside.   The contrapposto
of the titian road   to the river at the left
and slope of the spanned   stream to the right
take us upward   to a tilting reservoir
beneath the steepled,   nebulous horizon.

[The Mona Lisa of the Backyard]
Lips parted,   parting words lost,
she'll stand for this   for seconds only.
Caught in the crook   of the car's open door,
she's pinned to this photo's   unsfumato backdrop:
a chain-link fence,   the cheerless reservoirs
of three galvanized   garbage cans.

This Still Life

—after Ted Hughes's "Secretary"

If I should touch her, she'd pause and, raising
an eyebrow, ask me what I meant: all
day like a question mark in a cryptic scrawl,
she poses in her wing chair, arching, bracing,

asserting her waves against stiff lines of thought.
Workday done, she straightens back and buttocks
like an exclamation point. Once home, she cooks
with basil and garlic the pasta wisely bought

at La Gioconda's shop, a proper dinner
for husband and children: dines, sits up straight
in her indicative mood, careful to hyphenate
this still life and mine at its latest epicenter.

Knowing her as I do . . . barely, if at all . . .
what's to explain a love so elliptical?

Open Houses

[in Pasadena]

The widow's house is so alive with death,
so quick with recollection that even I,
a stranger to the woman and her dead mate,
enter their voided lives as easily
as I awake and pull on in the morning
cold clothes dropped by the bed at night.

Everywhere are fossils of their intimate
lives: the tranquilizers for her midnight
bouts of disbelief in his impending death,
depressions in the chairs where every morning
they sipped their coffee and where at dusk I
contemplate their hummingbirds, uneasily.

[along the Gulf Coast]

Against the white and blue towel of sand and sky,
the houses glow like roses in the morning,
their pinks and creams absorbed at night,
leaving only the yellow frames I animate
in my shoreline drive, documenting at death
of day how we invade and inhabit so easily

the lives of strangers. We can say goodnight
to children we have not met and easily
drape an arm around our alien mate,
rinsing swimsuits at the sink. Like death,
life draws us to each other. We check the sky
as if to foretell the weather in the morning.

51

Women on Beaches

The women are glinting like knives
on the parched, immaculate beaches.

Their bodies bring to the beaches
the luminous promise of passion.

And tirelessly forwards and backwards,
the waves are assailing the women.

Yet the women are cool and reflective,
their eyes flat pools of silver,

their promise of passion a weapon,
the waves still rising and falling.

On Darkness, Teeth, and Lakes

1

I once spent a stretch of October nights under
the spell of a woman who lived, let's face
it, in a kind of hellhole and slept with her
screenless windows open, a loaded gun under
her Goodwill mattress, and in the wake of
Hurricane Kate, pine trees and power lines
down and a band of tornadoes predicted, I
drove across town to keep a second date with
a woman my therapist had already pegged
as human quicksand, and it's also true that I
went with one witty woman to a dinner party
and ate and laughed and stayed just to stay
with her, giving but a passing thought to the
brace of rottweilers roaming the house, their
nails clicking on the polyurethane floors like
ticklish bombs, but you, you make me
hesitate;

2

and, yes, I said yes to bird watching at Saint
Marks one frangible summer afternoon,
letting no one I knew lead me for miles out
the narrow dikes between canals filled with
cottonmouths and alligators, letting the day
die, the sunset stymie and strand us, reducing
our world to the agitated beam of her flashlight
and the paired red lights of the alligators' eyes,

all because I liked the lean look of her and
thought I might like her, too, growing even
surer as she led me back through the darkness,
squeezing my hand tighter each time
we crossed the alligator runs, places along
the path where the tall grass on either side lay
flattened by the jurassic traffic pulsing
between the canals, but you, you make me
hesitate, stop and think;

3

and, once, on my birthday, unmoored by the
champagne shared on the dock, I climbed
into a canoe, water terror be damned, with a
soul more runic than Lake Bradford's flat,
anthracitic face, no life preserver on or on
board, the clubhouse closing, the lightning
already engraving the slab of sky above, velvety
drapes of rain in the offing, and one year later,
had I grown any wiser? of course not, just older,
so there I was, tempting Lake Seminole with
the only woman at the bar just two nights
earlier who *did* not/*could* not drink, now
drunk, her Evinrude harrowing the lake, as
she steered us through a crop of visible
cypress stumps, heedless of all the laggards
just beneath the surface, but you, you make me
hesitate, stop and think, perseverate . . .
on darkness, teeth, and lakes,
on edges and emptiness.

Triolet on the Opening Lines of the Green River Killer's Holographic Apology for Murdering Forty-Eight Women

I'm sorry for killing all those young ladys.
I have tried hard to remember as much as I could.
The first of my clusters goes back to the eighties.
I'm sorry for killing all those young ladys—
and raping their corpses on return trips to Hades
(I hid some in the water, far more in the woods).
I'm sorry for killing all those young ladys.
I have tried hard to remember as much as I could.

The Only Ones

Well they'd made up their minds to be everywhere because why not.
Everywhere was theirs because they thought so.
—W. S. Merwin, "The Last One"

Well if there were a buzz in nature
they wouldn't hear it
because how could they?
Everywhere was theirs because they made it so.

They wouldn't hear the busy legs of insects
turning the dead leaves, feathers oaring the air,
fly wings thinning it.
They would hear nothing above the scrape
of their Hi-Tecs on mapped paths,
whispers of Gore-Tex, crisp rips of Velcro
unleashing their mail-order gadgetry,
any means to leave the beeloud glade,
binoculars, smartphones, such things.
Everywhere was theirs because they made it so.

Well if death were near them
they wouldn't smell it
because why would they?
Everywhere was theirs because they said so.

On the rush-hour buses traveling north
through the city, every seat stuffed
with private remains and in the aisles
more bodies hanging,
they will be loudtalking to friends
who cannot wait to call or be called,
their merry voices laving the wildlife around them,

shoeless psychotics, Night Train riders,
the impaled children buried in their clothes.
Everywhere was theirs because they said so.

Well if they were to wake in a gray meadow
they wouldn't see it
because what of it?
Everywhere was theirs because nowhere was.

From their cockpits and crow's nests,
they see the usual everything nothing.
Surrounding Sound and sky
drained of the blue hues,
buildings bleached and blending
with the sky so what,
their thoughts will not turn to desolate interstates,
static and steam, webs of the tent caterpillars
binding the branches of the roadside trees.
Everywhere was theirs because nowhere was.

In Its Every Drop and in All Its Parts

What happens in a fountain and in its every drop happens also in a building
and in all its parts . . . . What goes up must come down: gravity reasserts
itself after the initial impulse is exhausted . . . .
—Claude Bragdon, *The Frozen Fountain* (1932)

Waiting at the bank of elevators
off the pedestrian retail rotunda,

the sound of the fountain receding,
the successes mass for the rapture.

Cued by the twin bursts of light
and sound, the proven prophecy

of the opening of another burnished,
vanishing door, they press forward,

execute their graceless one-eighties
to stand shoulder to shoulder,

expectant in the express elevator,
the brushed gold of its interior

giving each occupant a featureless,
fraternal twin, creating a second

mute choir of morticians bearing
identical burdens—briefcases,

coffee cups, the sad sheet music
no one has time to read anymore.

After the nervous eternity spent
arranging themselves, settling in,

they are grateful for that gentle
jolt that sets the vault in motion.

Gathering speed as they're swept
through the twenty bypassed floors,

they feel both lighter and wearier.
Who isn't indulging the fantasy?

What a relief it would be to drop
everything and exhale, slip out of

these perfectly ridiculous coats,
say to hell with these silent parts.

Why not talk? Why not sing?
Why not keep going, converge, be

out of time in a good way for once?
But the express dwindles to a local,

the stops and departures begin,
and another dreadful day unfolds

for the briskly exiting passengers
and their invisible stalker twins.

Down they all go at day's end,
when gravity reasserts itself.

Dinner on Lake Washington

At your special window table,
everything's going your way.
Why, here comes the sommelier
with the captain's list,
and the sated moon
could not be brighter
above the lake,
its beams afloat
atop the soft sable.
The jetskis and pleasure boats
tethered in the marina below
look well fed and rested,
and your lucky guests
could not be more delighted
as Tim, your lucky waiter, replaces
with weightless crystal
the ordinary wineglasses
the ordinary patrons lift
to their unenchanted lips.
The uncountable lights
in the brass spray
of the chandelier
have dropped into your glass,
reminding you of the golden eyes
of the peacock's tail
displayed for you alone
as you crossed the grounds
of the winery that very afternoon.
Appraising your splash
of Cherryblock Cabernet
as though seeking some fortune
in the whirlpool of the glass,
you give your approving nod,

and later when the grated
white pepper meets
your salad's needs,
you need only nod
once more and nod
again as you cut into
your twelve-ounce
New York Strip,
confirming the precise hue
you had requested.

But what is this? Somewhere
between the marinated mushrooms
and the espresso and port,
the fickle moon has flashed
high above your window,
its beams no longer bathing the lake
but casting instead
a jittery blanket of sparks
over the rolling darkness,
maddeningly hyphenating the lake,
and the boats lashed to the dock
are no longer rocking
in time with each other,
but thrashing about as though
some famished creature
had been loosed for sport
among them.

Beyond the lake,
on the hill of Medina,
where the primordially

wealthy live, oblivious
to you and your good fortune
in just being alive,
in having survived it all,
the lights are likewise aflicker,
and you can see
that to them
the opposite side of the lake,
where you and your satisfied
friends are waiting,
is likewise a bed of embers.

You slip your credit card
inside the leather folder
that Tim has so
graciously placed
at your elbow.

One Zennish Adonic, Skin of a Bubble

Back when I was a poet, moonlight could wake me,
blasting through its borehole in the firmament.
I was so fragile then, a breeze could break me.

I'm blast-proof now. Rays can't penetrate me.
I sleep like a stone, blind to all signs of impermanence,
though back when I was a poet, moonlight could wake me.

Driving through the dark rain, headlights strafing me,
I was shell-shocked by traffic lights, volatile ornaments.
I was so fragile then, a breeze could break me.

Life's safer on autopilot. Nothing shakes me:
not midnight, not lightning, no transit through turbulence.
Yet back when I was a poet, moonlight could wake me,

and one zennish adonic, *skin of a bubble,* could make me
perseverate for days on the earth's impermanence.
I was so fragile then, a breeze could break me.

Now I get and spend. Words don't agitate me.
My skin is a hide, all my senses impervious,
though back when I was a poet, moonlight could wake me:
I was so weightless then, a breeze could take me.

IV. Above

Split Couplet on Same

I know it could be an enveloping blue flame,

black water rushing through a car window,
bright blood, then snow,

some seaside resort in *Delta Sky* magazine,
or a cryptic scene

in a dream from which I cannot shake my life free;
or it could be

the punctured ceiling tiles in a hospital room,
a dahlia's bloom,

or beneath it a snarl of earthworms as I weed
the garden you buried

in the spring. Please let it be you, those gray eyes
that hypnotize

my senses, sating them, making me feel less hollow,
less blasted, though

blowing me away all the same.

The VFW Post 3308 Cemetery

Below the lake well fed by Munson Slough,
the coffins shift and sway in the aqueous plots
of a Panhandle cemetery cut from a pine stand.
The six-foot granite slabs, arranged like cots

in some disaster ward, are stretched across
the percolating soil as if to anchor
underground this drowned fleet of brass-
trimmed barks. But from this hopeless harbor,

no one's setting sail: no need to pack
the jeweled hilt, the helm and shield, the golden
tokens for the Otherworld. No distant Western
Isles will beckon this grim cargo of broken

bones and infected flesh. Not ships, but cradles
bear the dead, rocking their scrubbed and rubbery
bodies, dressed in dreams of life, like someone's
this or that, into a sleep that history

cannot reach, the insensate presents of dolls.
On this gray day, along the graveled shoal
between the rows of sinking graves, who
has time for this lost lot, this foreign soil?

From a half mile away arise the wet
slap and shush of tires on the two-lane road
running from Tallahassee to the happy coast,
urging us to take the wheel and look to windward.

Resolution

As a young man,   matchless wrecker
of cars and hearts,   cutter and carver
of North Georgia marble;   in middle age
a workman in plaster   and wood, maker
of the pearly, gold-   cuffed praying hands
and tables with lathe-   turned, tapering legs;

as an old man,   master of the Polaroid
and pointilism by number,   liberator of the inter-
locking rings,   king of jigsaw,
Cryptoquote,   crosswords, and Jumble:

now finished at last,   the final piece
solidly placed   in the solitary puzzle
of his young grave   (the yellow jackets
humming among   the mums, indecipherable).

Séance, a Vision for the One Shipping Out

Someday, when you are resoundingly dead
and your legacy has shrunk to a stray shred

or two of the good stuff randomly buried
under sofa cushions and your mark's preserved

only in the browning margins of dated textbooks
your acidic living fingers took you through

or in the cracked and fading seal of a T-shirt
now used to dust the table where you worked,

your fast friends will be dining round that table,
dreamily swirling their plummy Syrah, incapable

of recalling you, your place already assumed
by one you'd known only as a name she knew;

then someone will forge a signature word or phrase,
conjuring, from the faithless candlelight, your face.

Of the Tibetan Lion Dog

For young Jack is a small lion in my house.
—Hunt Hawkins, "My Cat Jack"
For there is the Thunder-Stop, which is the voice of God direct.
—Christopher Smart, "Of the Spiritual Musick"

For the parts of the Tibetan lion dog are as follows:
For the heart is murmurous but sound;
For the head is a chrysanthemum nuzzling the tall grass, but softer,
        more smellable yet;
For the nose leather is black, polished, and the shelf of the nose
        precise;
For the fleecy, white bellyhair seems edible to children;
For the torso is a stretched and sturdy monument when the lion dog
        guards our house, sphinx of the sliders;
For the right forepaw of the sphinx is precious paw, ever curled to
        the pettable chest;
For the tremor in the neck is both theatrical and worrisome;
For the pituitary tumor is a goad to the adrenal glands;
For the tail is a plume but in her last days ratskinned;
For the golden coat is now sparse, the keratoses not;
For the pancreas is a vindictive organ, furious with fat;
For the flux is pure blood;
For the blood is the blood of Paper Dragon and Yobo Ting-Yay, of
        Sonny Boy, Spot, and Judy, of the ancestral palace pets;
For the teeth are as sharp as my conscience;
For the eyes are on me as the lion dog roars and relaxes.

This Cell of All Places

So you have to go inside because
everyone says you should so this you
do and then it's all up to you to find
the right name the right door when
there are stacks and rows of doors
but this you do and then once more
you go inside and speak your name
into the glass room inside the room
inside the place you had to go inside
because everyone said you should
and wait some more as you were told
to do until you're called and led to a
smaller room to wait some more and
this you also do because well you
imagine everyone would still say you
should so in you go and become
upon request because why not what's
it going to hurt it won't kill you a
wholly naked thing surrendering
your malleable layers for this
crackling paper sheet your chair for
this papered workbench where
there's nothing for you to do until
someone comes to work on you but
wait some more as you were told to
do so of course you do and all the
while there's nothing at all for you to
do except study the posters tacked to
the wall blowups from some biology
textbook displaying all the
formidably low-tech machinery of
the thorax and the abdomen with its

dear god lurid mess of this and that
and god knows what all and god
knows what it all means or why you
must repeat the words *duodenum
jejunum duodenum jejunum* fit them
inside your most private prayer
*duodenum jejunum duodenum
jejunum in nomine patris et filii et
spiritus sancti* until you feel lost
there but what the hell you'll stay
because now you know there's
always something inside of
something no end to this no place
where you can go stop rest keep
yourself whole so you are sure now
how could you not be when everyone
said you should come here that
something new will be found inside
of you some ghostly glow already
there inhabiting you as beyond the
lonely window the sunbreak is
already there brightening the lines
between the blinds slicing the
pinned-up torso on the wall like an
appalling loaf of bread that nobody
wants to eat and you know as you
face the sun that at your back the
Oort Cloud rolls and beyond it lie the
black intragalactic spaces and farther
out everything discoverable now and
forevermore extending even unto the
iridescent inner walls of this

capacious droplet leaving you to
wonder why everyone said you
should come here and go inside the
room inside the room and stay here
growing older and older colder and
colder beneath your paper shroud in
this cell of all places.

Anchoress

Last night,
she dreamed
the horizon

was a ridge
of flame,
a perfect

repetition
of orange
triangles

defining
the serrated,
perforated

line
where heaven
was ripped

from earth.

She saw
the globe
as one glabrous

baby's
head
crowned

in fire
and watched
as the crown

grew tighter
and tighter
as time

was added
to time
to grow

shorter
and shorter
until

she could smell
that violent
crown

searing
the temples
of human-

kind.

Today
she woke
to see

the common
royalty,
the queens

and kings
of the ends
of things

sailing
past
her grate

in their impossible
burning
crowns,

and she
despaired
that none

was troubled
by the weight
and none

yet aware
of the stern
smell

in the air
of burnt
hair

and flesh.

Plain Sailing

The whole secret is in getting the first hand freed; after that,
it is all plain sailing.
—Harry Houdini, "How I Effect My Rope Escape,"
    San Francisco Examiner (June 19, 1899)

Lashed to a chair in a hive of rope,
screened in his ghost house,

he lets his aped-out muscles relax,
pushes his last breath out.

Twisting, shifting, he senses the slack,
sending it in a steady wave

to his near hand, and like *that,* he's back,
strutting downstage,

hands raised in greeting like the Pope
(one forearm slightly chafed,

but ulnar nerves and wrist bones intact,
no trace of wooden splinters

along his arms or down his back).
When those who paid to see

that feat hungered for rougher seas,
a higher-stakes escape,

he tucked himself, stripped and cuffed,
into the steel cocoon

of a milk can tested on stage with an ax
and filled past full with water.

Failure means a drowning death!
this latest trap was touted,

but behind sham rivets at the collar
was a simple sliding latch.

Bypassing the padlocked top,
out he springs, smacks

the cuffs against the galvanized hull,
replaces the generous hat.

When the encircling curtain drops,
he's posing before his tomb,

barefoot in a modest pool of water,
seal-slick arms spread wide.

Not all applaud when he reenters.
For some, it's not nearly enough.

They'd like to nail him to his seat
and pull the rope so tight

his biceps bleed, or take such a whack
at the steel the bolt won't slide.

The whole secret, after all, is in getting
the skeptics to swallow the swap,

accept spectacle as miracle,
take craft for art, forgetting

for a space that airtight vanishing act
of a vessel once grazing the sea.

Water Witch

It's a dirty tree, our splintery neighbor said,
of the forked madrona standing just within

our line, and it *is* lousy with leaf spots, but veiled
beneath that peeling hide is cinnamon skin,

and with roots that can break bedrock for water,
that tree can thrive anywhere and forever.

Fish Spine

—after Eliot Porter's *Balsam Spruce Forest* (May 11, 1968)

A
tall
slate
fish spine with
ribs
disturbingly
slanted is
crumbling
and climbing
still
in crippled
crosses, ladder-
like
through the blue
mists,
dying, picked
clean
of green
growth and rising
still
in the spring-
bred forest
life
fed on
the stripped
limbs; hollow-
veined
and hovering,
the light-
wood

yet claims
the land-
scape, piercing
the sky,
a frail,
unfailing
shadow.

A November Meditation on the Long Nave

—from Latin *nāvis longa*, 'warship'

On a dark day,
take a slow walk
up the gray steps

through the westwork
down the long nave
to the rood screen

and the rose light.
Hear the footfalls
on the stone floors.

Hear the coins drop
in the alms box;
see the wicks glow

sending prayers home.
Is your heart healed
when you worship

in this soft light
on a dark day?
Take a step back,

cast your eyes up
to the ribbed hull
of the long nave:

may this warship
keeps your seas safe
through these dark days.

About the Author

M. B. Powell's poems have appeared in various journals, including *Atlanta Review, Dappled Things, The Lyric, Peregrine,* and *Third Wednesday,* and in the chapbook *Lovers, Mothers, Killers, Others.* The collection *Two Neutron Stars Collide; or, Everyone's Love Affair* is forthcoming in 2019. Recognition of individual poems includes *Atlanta Review's* International Poetry Contest Grand Prize (for "Phrases for Public Speakers at Sea"), the Princemere Poetry Prize (for "Slack Water"), and the Georgia Poetry Society's Educators Award (for "One Mother's Day"). Powell was a finalist in *Dogwood's* Annual Poetry Contest (for "Split Couplet on Same") and a runner-up for *America Magazine's* Foley Poetry Award (for "Of the Tibetan Lion Dog"), and she received a "Best of the Net" nomination from *Midway Journal* (for "Helicon Cracking"). Powell studied literature at Agnes Scott College (B.A.), the University of North Carolina at Chapel Hill (M.A.), and Columbia University (Ph.D.) and earned a J.D. from the University of Washington School of Law. She has taught at Florida State University, Saint Martin's University, and Pierce College and has published, as Marta Powell Harley, scholarly books, articles, and notes on medieval literature. Originally from Marietta, Georgia, she now lives in Union, Washington.

www.ingramcontent.com/pod-product-compliance
Lightning Source LLC
Chambersburg PA
CBHW031003090426
42737CB00008B/664